Living *in* Communion

Leray Heyne

Jesus Christ's CEOs Bible Institute is an equipping ministry of Windows of Heaven. JC CEOs**MEDIA** is an outreach ministry of Windows of Heaven.

Windows of Heaven Inc.

PO Box 27154

Anaheim Hills, CA 92809

jcceos.com

Dedication

Talk to any Jesus Christ's CEO *(man or woman)*, and they will tell you that the ministry of Windows of Heaven has been invaluable in equipping them to live experientially with the abiding presence of Jesus Christ through communion with God Holy Spirit.

But there is another that would argue they have benefited even more from this ministry than the owner themselves. Who are they? Spouses. Marriages have benefited greatly from the transformation that has taken place in JC CEOs, so much so that spouses have asked me to create content specifically for them.

This book fulfills that request. I dedicate Living in Communion to the spouses of Jesus Christ's CEOs.

Contents

Leading You Into Communion With God Holy Spirit

Chapter 1

Introduction

My parents and I were equal partners in Enjoy Food International. Around five years in, my dad retired, my Mom became the Chairman of the Board, and I became the President and CEO. As our company grew, we purchased another company to acquire its 45,000-square-foot manufacturing facility. This factory we needed desperately to continue our growth trajectory.

Mom and I had joining offices with a pass-through door. One afternoon she came through that door so mad, screaming, and shaking the Bible at me. "You need to read this!" she yelled. I yelled back at her, "I've tried multiple times. I don't understand it." She yelled back, "You need to try again!"

As a seven-year-old boy, I gave my life to Jesus Christ. As you can tell by this time in my life, Christ was not living in me, nor I in Him. (Galatians 2:20).

I share this so that you will have a picture of my starting point before Jesus drew me into a lifestyle of communion with Holy Spirit.

So let's recap.

I was a Christian, but Christ was not living in me, nor I in Him.

I was not reading the Bible, nor did I understand it.

I did not know that there was a God Holy Spirit.

"For everyone who asks receives, and he who seeks finds, and to him who knocks it will be opened." (Matthew 7:8, NKJV)

As I have already begun, I will continue to be transparent throughout this book. This way everyone reading this can have faith that if Jesus can lead me into living in communion with Holy Spirit with this as MY starting point, He can and will open the door to anyone who seeks Him as I do. (1 John 2:27)

Let me expand on this picture. What you're about to read no church, no man or woman, or best-selling author taught me. It was revealed to me by the Spirit. (1 Corinthians 2:10, Galatians 1:12) It's not that I didn't seek man's help. For over 15 years I went to two wonderful churches with pastors graced with prophetic and apostolic wisdom that I admired and desired immensely. (Ephesians 4:11–13)

On one occasion, the first pastor came to me and said, "Leray, as I pray for you, the Lord told me to just pray for you because there are things He's doing with you He will not tell me." I knew this to be true and knew the man had heard from the Lord. The next great man of God from my next church came to me one day and said, "Leray, the Lord showed me that He has taken you into His private chambers. I have never seen this for anyone before." I also knew this to be true and knew this man had heard from the Lord also. It's not that I didn't want help, but for some reason, in my case, Holy Spirit reserved me for Himself and prohibited others from participating with Him in teaching me a communion lifestyle in the Spirit. (John 14:26), (1 John 2:27)

Please don't misunderstand. I am not saying Holy Spirit didn't use these pastors or other people in my life. He most certainly did. But they were more like a drive-by. One person coming to my remembrance right now was a woman speaking at a marketplace conference in the mid-90s. From the pulpit she exhorted us by saying, "your lives would be much easier if you all could get this one truth. The truth is, you are all spirit beings having a human experience, not a human having a spiritual experience." (John 3:6, 1 Corinthians 6:17) With what Holy Spirit was trying to impart to me in that season of my life, this statement opened for me the windows of heaven's floodgates of understanding.

Another was a pastor whose ministry focused on the presence of God with us. (1 Corinthians 6:19) When Holy Spirit was teaching me this in His Word, I wasn't getting it. His impartation wasn't becoming my reality. This pastor lived with a profound reality of this truth and articulated it in a way that helped Holy Spirit make God's presence in us, upon us, and near us my new reality.

"And He Himself gave some to be apostles, some prophets, some evangelists, and some pastors and teachers, for the equipping of the saints for the work of ministry, for the edifying of the body of Christ, till we all come to the unity of the faith and of the knowledge of the Son of God, to a perfect man, to the measure of the stature of the fullness of Christ;" (Ephesians 4:11–13, NKJV)

Jesus Christ, without a doubt, has given grace gifts to apostles, prophets, evangelists, pastors, and teachers to equip the Saints. As you read further, you will learn that these equippers of the Saints have not led the Lord's people into communion with God Holy Spirit. And that tragedy has resulted in these church leaders not making authentic disciples of Jesus Christ.

This book leads the Church (Saints) into a lifestyle of communion with God Holy Spirit. It also is a resource for equippers of the Saints to lead their local churches into a lifestyle of communion with God Holy Spirit, which will result in their local assemblies being made into authentic disciples of Jesus Christ.

So let's get started with where this whole journey of living in communion with God Holy Spirit began for me and now being restored to the Universal Church.

Chapter 2

Holy Spirit Revealed

As of this writing, Teresa and I will celebrate our 42nd anniversary in two months. But back in year 15, we needed Jesus' mercy and compassion in our marriage. (Romans 9:15) At this same time the business was doing great, and I was winning awards as an elite CEO. I was living my dream and building a kingdom unto myself. The company had become my first love. Mom and Dad (my business partners) were so frustrated with me that they started praying this prayer.

Lord, do whatever it takes to bring
Leray into a personal relationship with you.

Simple, but as you will see, POWERFUL.

As Mom and Dad prayed, the Lord took His good hand off of me (Nehemiah 2:8). The business stopped prospering and because of our large overhead, the company, for the first time, suffered greatly.

The dream life I had designed and built for myself (or so I thought, LOL!) was a complete disaster. Now with Jesus Christ against me (Ezekiel 13:8, Ezekiel 29:3) I could do nothing; and believe me when I tell you I tried everything! Let's just say I have learned experientially that when the power and authority of Jesus Christ wants a door shut, no one can open it. When He wants one open, nobody can keep it shut. (Revelation 3:7)

"For to be carnally minded is death, but to be spiritually minded is life and peace. Because the carnal mind is enmity against God; for it is not subject to the law of God, nor indeed can be. So then, those who are in the flesh cannot please God."

(Romans 8:6–8, NKJV)

Teresa is the love of my life and the best gift Jesus has ever given me. But back in year 15, I was clueless that we had grown so far apart. Now add to that the company (my kingdom) was in so much trouble I didn't even know if we could make it from month to month. **I was desperate and started talking to God.**

One morning I opened the Bible to see if I could get some wisdom that would help me with my messed up carnal life. I think someone told me to start with John. If you read the Introduction, I didn't understand the Bible nor how the book of John was going to help me save my marriage and business. Then John 14:26 jumped right off the page!! Don't ask me how, but for the first time I had an understanding of scripture and what it was saying to me personally.

"But the Helper, the Holy Spirit, whom the Father will send in My name, He will teach you all things, and bring to your remembrance all things that I said to you."

(John 14:26, NKJV)

Instantly I had an understanding that Holy Spirit, whoever that was, could teach me all things (marriage, business, the Bible). I also understood that if I did not read the Word, how could this Holy Spirit bring back to my remembrance things He told me if I wasn't willing to let Him tell me?

This is the first verse Holy Spirit used to change my life. It is also the first verse I ever highlighted in my Bible. In fact, I didn't just highlight it. I boxed it to make it stand out.

From that day forward and for many years, I started every day by opening my Bible to John 14:26 and taking my right index finger and pounding it on the Bible, saying these words.

"You said, You said that Holy Spirit will teach me all things. I am here, now have Him teach me."

The fact that you are reading this is all the evidence you need to know that Jesus Christ answered my prayer. If you are willing, I will take you on the same journey Holy Spirit took me on and continues to take me on as He spiritually transforms me into the image of the fulness of Jesus Christ. (2 Corinthians 3:18)

Chapter 3

Reading the Bible

In the mid-90s, I was in (TEC) an international organization of CEOs. One month we had a speaker come in and perform a DISC strength assessment on each of us. The man went around the room and read everyone's results. When he got to me, he paused, looked puzzled, and said you're a borderline schizophrenic. The room literally fell on the floor laughing so hard, and then said, tell us something we don't already know.

The Strength Finder evaluated me as a creator and refiner. This meant my mind was in a constant tug-of-war with itself. The assessment identified that I refine faster than I create. In those days, my mind never, and I mean never, shut down, not even when I slept. I typically would come into the office each morning with new ideas or strategies, give them to my executive team and then frustrate them the next day because I had already refined them 10 times better before they even had a chance to execute them. They often asked me, "Do you ever sleep at night?"

I tell you this because someone reading this is going to say you don't understand. I do understand and do not want you to believe the lie that Holy Spirit, by the power and authority of Jesus Christ, cannot and will not take dominion over your body, heart, mind, soul, and spirit if you ask Him, just as I still do every day. Jude 25

OK? let's get back to my reality at this time in my life. My Mom had been telling me for years that I needed to read the Bible. Now

John 14:26 was also telling me this, so no matter how difficult I knew it was going to be, I knew I needed to do it. As you read on, you will learn how Holy Spirit had me approach two aspects of John 14:26. Here's a brief glimpse.

*"But the Helper, the Holy Spirit, whom the Father will send in My name, **[1] He will teach you all things,** and **[2] bring to your remembrance all things** that I said to you."*

(John 14:26, NKJV)

1. Holy Spirit will teach me all things.

Every day, I start my day in participation with Holy Spirit, seeking first the kingdom of God through the Word of God.
(Matthew 6:33)

2. Holy Spirit will bring to my remembrance all things

In addition, every day in participation with Holy Spirit, I use my journal to renew myself, letting Holy Spirit bring to my remembrance what He has already taught me through His Word.
(Romans 12:2)

Now, I have been very clear that I did not understand any of the Word of God before reading John 14:26, so how in the world did Holy Spirit give me an understanding as I read the Word of God?

Two words: Life-Circumstances!

Here's how I define Life-Circumstances. Anything and everything taking place in and around our life.

Over the years, I have said it like this. Holy Spirit has not used any one thing greater than business to reveal Jesus Christ to me. And He has not used anything more than Teresa, my wife, as a mirror to reveal the ugliness of my heart.

Holy Spirit taught me that I am His daily devotion.
I am the thing He wants to talk to me about every morning.

Chapter 4

Good Morning Lord

When I was in elementary school, my Mom was the alarm clock. She would come into my bedroom and say, "Son, it's time to get ready for school and have breakfast." Like Mom, Holy Spirit became my alarm clock. He would awaken me, and as I became conscious, I heard Him say, "Good morning, get up, I want to talk to you." I replied, "Good morning Lord, I want to talk to you too." Before, I was loving the Lord with my own desire to get up and read the Word every day. Holy Spirit knew I needed His help. The flesh was weak, and I wanted to sleep, but the Spirit was willing. (Mark 14:38) Our factory ran 24 hours a day, and our first shift started at 6 AM. I liked being at the office when that shift started, so that meant Holy Spirit was getting me up at 3 to 4 am. Once I was up, I really did love this season with the Lord.

Now that I was up, I would grab my coffee get to my desk and open my Bible and again say, "Good morning Lord, you know me better than I know myself, what do you want to talk to me about today?"

Here's how Holy Spirit answered me using my life circumstances.

Maybe He brought to my remembrance a fight I had with Teresa and showed me how angry I was. I knew He wanted to talk to me about anger. So I would open up my Bible concordance to find and read (seek) what the Bible had to say about anger. If there were 20 verses on anger, typically only two or three that morning would be speaking to me. Then I would drill down by reading and looking up their cross-references. Read other translations, and define key Words that were popping off the page. Then I would meditate on what Holy Spirit was teaching me in His Word and then journal "what I believed" God Holy Spirit was revealing to me and for me that morning.

On another day, maybe Holy Spirit would bring back to my remembrance a conversation I had with a vendor who was withholding a delivery because we couldn't pay them. So I knew the Lord wanted to speak to me about money and God's provision. So I may spend a week or longer studying (seeking) what the Word of God (Bible) had to say about Money and God's provision.

Now multiply this by seven days a week. You can imagine I am now starting to get around the Word of God quite a bit. So now Holy Spirit can bring back to my remembrance things He has already taught me in His Word. (John 14:26) For example, maybe I got angry again, and Holy Spirit said, "Hey, what have I taught you about the fruits of the Spirit?" Now, I know He's not happy with me, and He wants me to revisit the fruits of the Spirit. I do this by re-reading the Scriptures and using my journal to renew myself in previous Holy Spirit teachings regarding this subject. The Bible teaches us that this is renewing our mind so as not to be conformed or, in my case, remain conformed to this world. (Romans 12:2)

You get the idea. The Lord was using my life to contrast His way and my way. Holy Spirit was showing me how I was living life *(business, marriage, and as a man)* and then, through His Word, taught me how He wants me to live. In the beginning, I called this old way and new way and then learned the Bible teaches us that this is taking off the old man and putting on the new man. (Colossians 3:9–10)

Chapter 5

Journaling

In high school there was only one other subject I disliked more than English, and that was History. This resulted in me not being a good writer. I've always been perceived as a good communicator, but I didn't know how to structure my messages in writing. Therefore I had my Mom and assistant write my business correspondence back in the day. In addition, I was not a good speller and, therefore, couldn't read my own writing! So when I talk to you about the importance of journalling your private conversations with God Holy Spirit every day, you know this is not of my own doing.

"Again, in the ninth year, in the tenth month, on the tenth day of the month, the word of the Lord came to me, saying, "Son of man, write down the name of the day, this very day—the king of Babylon started his siege against Jerusalem this very day. And utter a parable to the rebellious house, and say to them, 'Thus says the Lord God: "Put on a pot, set it on, And also pour water into it."

(Ezekiel 24:1–3, NKJV)

The Lord spoke and told Ezekiel to **write down** and date what He said. In Hebrew, this simply means to make an administrative record.

"*In the first year of Belshazzar king of Babylon, Daniel had a dream and visions of his head while on his bed. Then he wrote down the dream, telling the main facts.*" (Daniel 7:1, NKJV)

The phrase **wrote down** in Hebrew gives insight into Daniel recording a memory of God's communication.

At this time of my life, writing was very difficult, and I did not enjoy it a bit. But when Holy Spirit led me as He did Ezekiel and Daniel to write down and date His instructions and correction so I would have a remembrance of them, it became easy and very enjoyable for me. God Holy Spirit was talking to me through His Word and about my life circumstances. I was listening and wanted to do and remember everything Holy Spirit was telling me.

"All Scripture is inspired by God and is useful to teach us what is true and to make us realize what is wrong in our lives. It corrects us when we are wrong and teaches us to do what is right. God uses it to prepare and equip his people to do every good work."

(2 Timothy 3:16–17, NLT)

By experience, I have learned that journaling Holy Spirit communications is a powerful tool He uses to write His Word on our hearts and mind, which perpetually transfoms us into a greater fullness of Jesus Christ. See Hebrews 8:10.

"For this is the covenant that I will make with the house of Israel after those days, says the Lord:
I will put My laws in their mind and write them on their hearts;
and I will be their God, and they shall be My people."

(Hebrews 8:10, NKJV)

Chapter 6

Seeking the Lord

Business owners, who are my sphere of influence, are typically disciplined individuals, and they take that attribute into everything in their life, including seeking the Lord. One afternoon I received a call from one of those business owners, who preceded to tell me how disciplined he is to get up and arrive at his office by 5 AM to seek the Lord first for six days a week. Immediately Holy Spirit gave me a word for this man.

"Brother, your discipline has been swallowed up by love. It is your love for the Lord, not discipline that compels you to get you up and spend time seeking the Lord first every day."

This man was so blessed that he wept and cried for the next ten minutes. He knew he loved the Lord (and by the way, so did all who knew this man) but he didn't realize, being a disciplined person, that it was now love and not discipline that was his passion to seek and know Jesus intimately. (Matthew 22:37–38)

Treasure Hunt

As Holy Spirit got me up to talk to me every morning, I started to become more and more like my friend. I was loving getting up to hear what Holy Spirit had to say to me. Back then and still today,

25 years later, seeking in communion with Holy Spirit is like being on an amazing treasure hunt, finding new treasure every morning. Here is what that treasure hunt looks like in communion with Holy Spirit.

"Yet to us God has unveiled and revealed them by and through His Spirit, for the [Holy] Spirit searches diligently, exploring and examining everything, even sounding the profound and bottomless things of God [the divine counsels and things hidden and beyond man's scrutiny]. For what person perceives (knows and understands) what passes through a man's thoughts except the man's own spirit within him? Just so no one discerns (comes to know and comprehend) the thoughts of God except the Spirit of God. Now we have not received the spirit [that belongs to] the world, but the [Holy] Spirit Who is from God, [given to us] that we might realize and comprehend and appreciate the gifts [of divine favor and blessing so freely and lavishly] bestowed on us by God. And we are setting these truths forth in words not taught by human wisdom but taught by the [Holy] Spirit, combining and interpreting spiritual truths with spiritual language [to those who possess the Holy Spirit]. But the natural, nonspiritual man does not accept or welcome or admit into his heart the gifts and teachings and revelations of the Spirit of God, for they are folly (meaningless nonsense) to him; and he is incapable of knowing them [of progressively recognizing, understanding, and becoming better acquainted with them] because they are spiritually discerned and estimated and appreciated."

(1 Corinthians 2:10–14, AMP)

How amazing is seeking the Lord! After reading this, how could you not want to get up every morning to spend time seeking the hidden things of God in communion with God Holy Spirit!

"If you seek her as silver, And search for her as for hidden treasures;"

(Proverbs 2:4, NKJV)

My mornings are the most precious and protected time of the day. I don't do anything until I spend private time with Holy Spirit so that I may know how to participate with Him throughout my day.

God is Love

"We have come into an intimate experience with God's love, and we trust in the love he has for us.
God is love! Those who are living in love are living in God, and God lives through them."

(1 John 4:16, TPT)

Saints, I don't know where you are at in your life right now, but what I do know is that Jesus Christ is no respecter of man. So just as my friend and I have done, if you will turn to the Lord with all of your heart, mind, soul, and strength, and say YES, and keep saying YES to Jesus for the rest of your life, love will immerse you and become the very source of your life.

Chapter 7

Meditation

Meditation in communion with Holy Spirit sounds really spiritual, doesn't it?

Let me let you in on a little secret, I didn't even know I was meditating at this point in my journey with Holy Spirit. In my time of seeking the Lord, all I was doing was taking my gifting, disciplines, and attributes for creating and refining into what I was reading in Scripture every morning. When you create, you mentally dwell on an idea over and over. You never stop thinking about it until you're at peace. And then, when you're refining an idea, your doubling down on all of that mental effort to understand and communicate the idea even better than before. In this section, you will learn what I have learned - every human being meditates, they just don't call it that.

Meditation Revealed

It was only a few years ago Holy Spirit revealed to me that every person meditates, they just don't call it that. Holy Spirit used a Jesus Christ CEO to enlighten me to this truth. This person is known in his local JC CEO community as a person who will never do that, and then, in a short period of time, Holy Spirit has him doing the very thing he said he wouldn't or couldn't ever do. Don't ever say never, LOL!

In one of our Tuesday morning meetings, this man looked across the table and said, "Leray, I am not like you or these other guys, with the way my mind works, I will never be able to meditate." Remember, he is talking to a former borderline schizophrenic whose mind never shut down! I immediately responded and said, "Brother, the Lord showed me that you already meditate, and you are probably 10 times better at it than all of us!" He replied, "how do I do that?"

"Every month as you prepare your client's billing, you scrutinize in great detail your team's work and accomplishments. You evaluate the team's work from the left and the right from the top and bottom. You spend hours pondering how you are going to articulate the Firm's added value before writing up the client's billing. You do this because your billings are quite large, and you want to have every possible question answered in advance in case your client disputes the billing." He looked at me and said, "I didn't even know you knew I did that!"

Then I asked him, "Brother, isn't this what you do?" he replied, "Yes!" I asked, "Are you good at it?" He humbly replied, "The best." I replied, "Yes, you are, and that's meditation! Now all you have to do is apply that same discipline to studying the Word of God in communion with Holy Spirit."

Breakthrough

It was only two weeks later when this JC CEO came into our Tuesday morning meeting and said, "Guys, you will be so proud of me. Last Saturday, I read and meditated on the Word of God for hours!" Then spent the rest of our meeting sharing all the revelation Holy Spirit imparted to him. You gotta love it, amen!!

The Benefits of Meditation

I want to share with you what King David says about the benefits of meditation.

"*Oh, how I love Your law! It is my meditation all the day. You, through Your commandments, make me wiser than my enemies; For they are ever with me. I have more understanding than all my teachers, For Your testimonies are my meditation. I understand more than the ancients, Because I keep Your precepts. I have restrained my feet from every evil way, That I may keep Your word. I have not departed from Your judgments, For You Yourself have taught me. How sweet are Your words to my taste, Sweeter than honey to my mouth! Through Your precepts I get understanding; Therefore I hate every false way. Your word is a lamp to my feet And a light to my path.*" (Psalm 119:97–105, NKJV)

King David shares that he loves meditating all day on God's Word, and it makes him wiser than all his enemies. Meditating gives him more understanding than all his teachers. And meditating on his experiential life (testimonies) gives him more understanding than those who are a lot older than him. Saints, Holy Spirit will teach you all things, and if you meditate on them, Jesus is no respecter of man, He will do for you what He did for King David. BELIEVE! (Matthew 17:20)

"Holy Spirit revealed to me that every person meditates, they just don't call it that."

Still don't believe it? Let me give you one last example for those of you with little faith and who are denying the power of God to bring you into a spiritual state of meditation. (Matthew 14:31)

"They profess to know God, but in works they deny Him, being abominable, disobedient, and disqualified for every good work."

(Titus 1:16, NKJV)

"having a form of godliness but denying its power. And from such people turn away!"

(2 Timothy 3:5, NKJV)

There is not one of you reading this that has not gotten into an argument with a close friend or family member. Then thought about that argument for hours, days, weeks, months, and maybe years. You have pondered every aspect of that argument. You have thought about the points you should've made but didn't make, things you should've said but didn't say, or things you said that you shouldn't have said. This kind of mental contemplation, pondering on a matter over and over, is meditation. Now that you see that you possess this discipline, apply it to studying the Word of God in communion with God Holy Spirit!

*"This kind of mental contemplation,
pondering on a matter over and over, is meditation."*

Please stop and pray this prayer before continuing.

Jesus, I believe but help my unbelief. I am asking for your dominion (manifest) presence and power to govern my body, heart, mind, soul, and spirit from this moment forward. By the power of Holy Spirit, please draw me into intimate times of meditation on your Word and how you want it applied in my life. And as you did with King David, make me wiser than Your enemies so that I may participate experientially with God Holy Spirit, manifesting your kingdom on earth to the standard that exists in heaven. In Jesus' name, amen (so be it).

See Matthew 6:10, Galatians 2:20, and Jude 25.

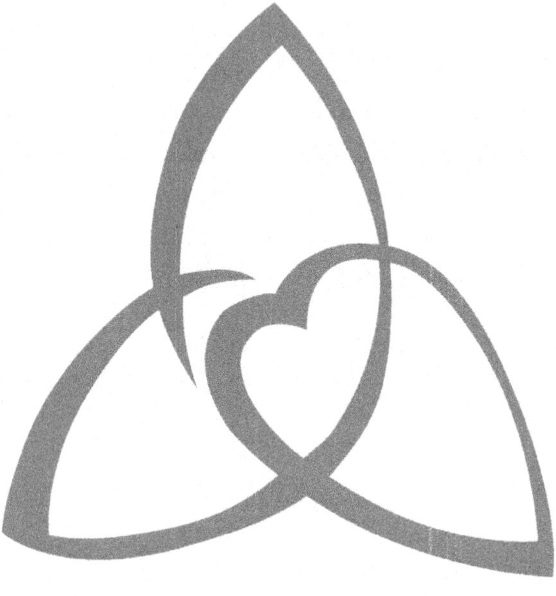

Chapter 8

Belief Exercise

As Holy Spirit reveals and teaches me every morning, I remember He would not let me confer with anyone to confirm that I was biblically sound in my understanding. He would ask me, "What do you believe?" as I journaled what I believed. He also asked me, "On a scale of one to ten, what is your belief in today's revelation?" Most of the time, it takes me many days of study and meditation to get my belief to a 10 on any one subject Holy Spirit is teaching me. Once I reached a 10, Holy Spirit tests that faith by exercising my belief through a life circumstance. I have learned by experience that there's nothing like life circumstances to test my heart and prove I don't fully believe God's Word at a 10!
See 1 Chronicles 29:17.

"But be doers of the word, and not hearers only, deceiving yourselves."

(James 1:22, NKJV)

Believing God's Word in my study closet is one thing. Living God's Word under the pressures of life is a whole other thing. I have learned by experience that Holy Spirit uses life circumstances to exercise our belief experientially as part of His method of revealing Jesus Christ, the righteousness of God, and adding to our faith.

"I have learned by experience that there's nothing like life circumstances to test my heart and prove I don't fully believe God's Word at a 10."

What is 'Belief Exercise'?

Let's say Holy Spirit has already accounted to you a degree of faith in money, God's provision. Maybe you have attained faith in God's financial provision for one month or even a year. But on the 366th day, with no provision provided, you shrink back and become 'of little faith.' The 366th day becomes the new beginning point to "add" to the faith Holy Spirit has already accounted to you. In our Christian communities, we would revere this person as a person with great faith. But Holy Spirit knows He is not even close to being finished in revealing Christ and adding to a person's faith no matter how much faith and revelation He has already accounted to them.

"For in it the righteousness of God is revealed from ***faith to faith;*** *as it is written, "The just shall live by faith."*

(Romans 1:17, NKJV)

Ok, here's another example. Let's say you can benchpress 100 pounds but want to be able to benchpress 200 pounds. So you exercise with increased weight *(pressure)* over a period of time, then eventually, you are able to benchpress 200 pounds. I have learned by experience that this is how the Holy Spirit uses the pressures of life circumstances to increase our revelation and faith to a greater degree than He has already accounted to us in any particular truth/promise.

Red Line

Over the years as a business owner, I have had thousands of life circumstances where I required cash, not provision, but real money to solve my situations. Because of these thousands of opportunities, the Lord has given me great faith in finances. So much so that one day, I told the Lord I don't need another sign, and I will never ask you for faith for finances again. This declaration of faith shows you the faith Holy Spirit had accounted to me up until that point, but He wasn't done adding to my faith. He immediately teed up a very difficult life circumstance to continue to add to the faith He had already accounted to me.

To do this, the Lord led me into a long season, 5 years, where Teresa and my income was only 40% of what our monthly household requirements were. This led to the bank wanting to foreclose on our home. The simple solution was to sell the home, take the $250,000 in equity and start over. But in my seeking time with the Lord, Holy Spirit said, "Do not sell the house for I have created a path of deliverance for you." This is where my 'belief exercise' kicked in, and it required me for years to persevere and endure exercising my belief (faith) in what I believed Holy Spirit told me.

The pressure from creditors was great. The criticism from Christian family members and friends was even greater. They wanted me to take the simple way out: sell the house, take the equity, and start over. But Holy Spirit was challenging me to believe Him over their wise counsel. From their perspective, it was black or white, I was thoroughly wrong, and they were much obliged to give me cherry-picked scriptures to prove it! I remember telling a ministry partner while crying like a baby, I want to be a man that can go the full distance with the Lord, I don't want nor can handle starting this faith-to-faith test over again because I gave up on the one-yard line.

Let's fast forward. The week of my birthday, our house went into foreclosure, and we received a demand letter to surrender the home to the bank. I had just gone past the mortgage industry's 'red line' and had become the fool everyone said I was. Or had I?

On my birthday, I was out to lunch with a good friend. He did not know we were on the brink of losing our home. I told him what had been going on in our lives. He said, "Let me talk to my Dad, he helps people in situations like yours." My friend's Dad is a very wealthy and benevolent Christian. I had never met him, so he wasn't part of my immediate sphere of influence. As promised over the weekend, my friend presented our situation to his Dad, and on Monday, his Dad stepped in and brought our mortgage current, paid off the second, made our house payment for the next 12 months, and because I was in full-time ministry, I did not need to start making payments until the 13th month. This cash miracle (interest-free loan) totaled $150,000!!

This was the Lord's path of deliverance for me and what it means to fully and thoroughly exercise your belief (faith), persevering and enduring at a 10 while under the pressures of life circumstances.

The Lord has a history of declaring a timeframe to accomplish His will. If you don't believe me, do an Old Testament Bible search on 40 years, and you will see that this is true. In my case, Jesus declared that I must cross the mortgage industry 'red line' before He would have Holy Spirit reveal the path of deliverance He had waiting for me.

To wrap up the story, 13 months into the loan, Teresa and I refinanced the house and paid off my friend's Dad in full. We also were able to build in our backyard the custom rock pool and spa Teresa dreamed of and that I had promised her for 25 years. Thank you, Lord, for drawing up life circumstances to experientially increase my and Teresa's revelation and faith in Jesus. Our deliverer!

"And it will be said in that day: "Behold, this is our God;
We have waited for Him, and He will save us.
This is the Lord; We have waited for Him;
We will be glad and rejoice in His salvation."

(Isaiah 25:9, NKJV)

Signs and Wonders

I have witnessed that almost every Christian wants signs and wonders to follow their lives, but they're not willing to let Jesus lead them into life circumstances where they need those miracles. They are no different than Israel was in Moses' day. Here are three excerpts from the Red Sea story.

"So ***God led the people*** *around by way of the wilderness of the Red Sea. And the children of Israel went up in orderly ranks out of the land of Egypt."*

(Exodus 13:18, NKJV)

"And when Pharaoh drew near, the children of Israel lifted their eyes, and behold, the Egyptians marched after them. ***So they were very afraid****, and the children of Israel cried out to the Lord."*

(Exodus 14:10, NKJV)

"And Moses said to the people, "Do not be afraid. ***Stand still, and see the salvation of the Lord, which He will accomplish for you today****. For the Egyptians whom you see today, you shall see again no more forever."*

(Exodus 14:13, NKJV)

If you are living the Galatians 2:20 lifestyle, where it's no longer you who live but it's Christ living in you, then He is going to lead you into life circumstances greater than anything you can imagine. If you have prayed (Ephesians 3:20), then you need to realize Holy Spirit answers your prayer by using life circumstances as one of His methods of revealing the power that works in you abundantly and exceedingly above anything you can imagine or ask. So please stop being afraid and let (trust) His abundant power and authority manifest in you, bearing witness to the world that you are an authentic disciple of Jesus Christ. (Mark 16:17–18)

Precious Stones

By the way, this is how precious stones are also made. Do you know that the Lord calls you a precious, living stone? Have you ever considered how precious stones are made?

"Come to Him [then, to that] Living Stone which men tried and threw away, but which is chosen [and] precious in God's sight. [Come] and, like living stones, be yourselves built [into] a spiritual house, for a holy (dedicated, consecrated) priesthood, to offer up [those] spiritual sacrifices [that are] acceptable and pleasing to God through Jesus Christ."

(1 Peter 2:4–5, AMP)

Precious stones are made by going through treatments of cutting, polishing, heat, radiation, waxing, and fracture filling. It's these types of applied pressures that make stones precious. You are the Lord's precious living stone. The intensity and length of a life circumstance are simply an opportunity to exercise your belief in order to increase you from faith to faith and that it may be made complete in Jesus Christ. Rejoice in life circumstances always, again I say, rejoice! (1 Thessalonians 5:16)

Feature

GOD KNOWS
WHAT HE'S ABOUT!

When God wants to drill a man
And thrill a man
And skill a man
When God wants to mold a man
To play the noblest part;
When He yearns with all His heart
To create so great and bold a man
That all the world shall be amazed,
Watch His methods, watch His ways!
How He ruthlessly perfects
Whom He royally elects!
How He hammers him and hurts him,
And with mighty blows converts him
Into trial shapes of clay which
Only God understands;
While his tortured heart is crying
And he lifts beseeching hands?
How He bends but never breaks
When his good He undertakes;
How He uses whom He chooses
And with every purpose fuses him;
By every act induces him
To try his splendor out-
God knows what He's about!

-Author Unknown

Chapter 9

Experiences

Spiritual Experiences are my absolute favorite aspect of living in communion with Holy Spirit. Here's why. Every time I exercise a belief in a life circumstance, I experience *(discern)* a spiritual reality with Holy Spirit that increases my understanding and surpasses the knowledge I gained in my time of study and meditating on the Word alone. The Word of God teaches us that this is true for all believers.

"..that Christ might finally settle down and feel completely at home in your hearts through your faith; in love having been firmly rooted and grounded in order that you may be able to grasp with all the saints what is the breadth and width and height and depth, and ***to know experientially the love of Christ which surpasses experiential knowledge*** *in order that you may be filled up to the measure of all the fulness of God."*

(Ephesians 3:17–19, WUESTNT)

I love the Greek scholar Kenneth Wuest's translation, he makes it so clear. Apart from experiencing the abiding presence of Jesus Christ through communion with Holy Spirit, Christians cannot possess a full revelation of the love of God nor be filled up to the measure of the fullness of God.

Remember, before the Lord drew me into my 'red line' mortgage circumstance, I already had great faith in finances. I already knew God's Word and experienced it over many years in thousands of business circumstances requiring the Lord's provision. But unbeknownst to me, the Lord was going to put me into full-time ministry and not provide an income to me for 14 years! This was going to require faith in God's promises to provide to a degree that I had not already attained to. This was not the Lord being cruel, but rather putting on the new man and taking off the old man. See, my old man was very good at making money and leveraging everybody else's money, and selling anything to anyone. But Holy Spirit was preparing me to be an overseer of one of Jesus' Storehouses which called for a deeper transformation in my heart.

"For our gospel did not come to you in word only, but also in power, and in the Holy Spirit and in much assurance, as you know what kind of men we were among you for your sake."

(1 Thessalonians 1:5, NKJV)

Simply reading, studying, and meditating on the Word of God will not bring about a complete revelation or transformation in the fullness of Jesus Christ. We must ***experience the living Word in power*** through our participation in the abiding presence of Jesus Christ through communion with God Holy Spirit! This goes beyond mere academic knowledge of Jesus. (Hebrews 4:12)

Experiencing Jesus' Presence

"Do not lie to one another, since you have ***put off the old man*** *with his deeds, and have* ***put on the new man*** *who is renewed in knowledge according to the image of Him who created him,"*

(Colossians 3:9–10, NKJV)

What is the old man? Simply put, flesh or carnal. What is the new man? One who is born of the Spirit and thereby one spirit with God.

"That which is born of the flesh is flesh,
and that which is born of the Spirit is spirit."

(John 3:6, NKJV)

"But you are not in the flesh but in the Spirit, if indeed the Spirit of God dwells in you. Now if anyone does not have the Spirit of Christ, he is not His. And if Christ is in you, the body is dead because of sin, but the Spirit is life because of righteousness. But if the Spirit of Him who raised Jesus from the dead dwells in you, He who raised Christ from the dead will also give life to your mortal bodies through His Spirit who dwells in you."

(Romans 8:9–11, NKJV)

"But he who is joined to the Lord is one spirit with Him."

(1 Corinthians 6:17, NKJV)

Living this lifestyle in communion with Holy Spirit, as I am describing, will lead all Christians into an experiential reality of the living and abiding presence of Jesus Christ in them as temples of the Holy Spirit. (2 Corinthians 1:*22*)

I believe with all of my heart that as the body of Christ lives from a conscious reality of the abiding presence of Jesus Christ in communion (participation) with God Holy Spirit, it will absolutely change everything in the Universal Church as we and the world view it today.

"I have been crucified with Christ; it is no longer I who live,
but Christ lives in me; and the life which I now live in the flesh I
live by faith in the Son of God,
who loved me and gave Himself for me."

(Galatians 2:20, NKJV)

Most Christians look at challenging life circumstances as problems or attacks from the devil. I view and look at all life circumstances as I'm about ready to receive, experience, and be perfected by and with Holy Spirit:

- a greater revelation of the manifold wisdom of God. (Ephesians 3:10)
- a greater revelation of the exceedingly abundant power of the abiding presence (love) of Christ in me. (Ephesians 3:20)
- a greater fullness of Jesus Christ. (John 17:23, Ephesians 4:13)

I hear Christians make this statement all the time, and quite frankly, I just don't get it. *"I can't wait for Jesus to come."*

Saints, I'm having so much fun with Jesus right now, I hope He waits. We have eternity with Christ, but we only get one shot to participate with Him in this world. In this regard, I pray that all Saints will be like me. I'm not interested in only knowing the theology of Jesus Christ. I am more interested in knowing Him intimately as God, a friend, my lover, my everything. As the apostle Paul taught us in Ephesians, and as the Greek scholar gives insight, this is impossible apart from having an experiential reality of Jesus' abiding presence with us at all times.

This is why spiritual experiences are my favorite aspect of living in communion with God Holy Spirit. I am praying that it becomes yours.

Chapter 10

Discernment

One of the most common requests among new Christians is to hear God's voice, and I, too, had this desire as I began reading John 14:26. I want you to know that Holy Spirit desires you to hear His voice even more than you want to hear Him. If you habitually live in communion with Him, I can assure you, you'll be able to discern very well the various ways in which He communicates with those who are led by His Spirit.
(Romans 8:14, Galatians 5:25)

Here's how that journey began for me. As you know, Holy Spirit woke me up every morning. During my private time with Him, and as He guided me through the Word and taught me, I kept having thoughts about business. Since I had a passion for business, I assumed these ideas were trying to distract me from my time with the Holy Spirit. However, one day the Holy Spirit asked me a question.

First, Holy Spirit reminded me that He had taught me that it's no longer I who live, but it's Christ living in me. (Galatians 2:20)

And I was bought at a price, and my life is not my own but a temple of the Holy Spirit. (1 Corinthians 6:19) Then Holy Spirit asked this thought-provoking question, ***"As you faithfully sit with me and let me teach you, what makes you think any of your thoughts are your own?"*** WOW, what a revelation for me, and I hope it will be for you too.

Pause

I want you to pause right now and meditate on this thought. If it's no longer you who lives but Christ living in you as a temple of the Holy Spirit, what makes you think any of your thoughts are your own?

See, before I recognized Holy Spirit was using business to give me an understanding of God's Word and using business life circumstances to reveal Himself to me, I thought all the business thoughts I was having were my own. I didn't realize Holy Spirit was speaking to me about business, and it was Him showing me how I was doing business versus how He wanted me to do business according to His will. (old man/new man)

Just like the young Samuel, from that moment forward, everything changed for me. (1 Samuel 3) By faith, I said to myself, yeah, what makes me think any of my thoughts are my own as I sit here genuinely seeking (learning, talking, and listening) to God Holy Spirit? For a long season thereafter, I came out of my prayer closet with Holy Spirit's correction and instruction; a to-do list that I was to exercise at work every day. (2 Timothy 3:16–17)

"But the natural man does not receive the things of the Spirit of God, for they are foolishness to him; nor can he know them, because they are spiritually discerned."

(1 Corinthians 2:14, NKJV)

Question

I want you to think about this question. How did I and how will you become more proficient at spiritual discernment, spiritually mature in perceiving God Holy Spirit's communication imparted by His Spirit?

Answer

You must live intentionally in communion with Holy Spirit, **seeking**, **meditating**, **journaling**, and **exercising belief** in the Spirit and by the Spirit. Then by **experience**, you will trust Holy Spirit's abiding presence more and more.

Don't believe it yet? Let me share this truth with you in a couple of other ways.

Exercise, Long Usage

*"For everyone who partakes only of milk is unskilled in the word of righteousness, for he is a babe. But solid food belongs to those who are of full age, that is, those who **by reason of use** have their senses exercised to discern both good and evil."*

(Hebrews 5:13–14, NKJV)

*"For everyone whose sole diet is milk, is inexperienced in a message which is righteous in quality, for he is a [spiritually] immature person. But solid food belongs to those who are [spiritually] mature, **to those who on account of long usage** have their powers of perception exercised to the point where they are able to discriminate between both that which is good in character and that which is evil."*

(Hebrews 5:13–14, WUESTNT)

When reading these two translations side-by-side, we learn that those who do not live in communion with Holy Spirit are inexperienced and spiritually immature people. We have also learned that those who intentionally engage in having their senses exercised over long periods of time become spiritually mature by having their perceptions exercised to the point where they're able to discriminate between what is of Holy Spirit, their flesh, or evil principalities.

Through the Word of God, we see there are no shortcuts. Jesus (God) makes the rules on how man will come to know and be in a relationship with Him. If you are not willing to live in communion with God Holy Spirit and on His terms, then don't expect to know Him or His communications by the Spirit.

"Now the Lord is the Spirit, and where the Spirit of the Lord is, there is freedom."

(2 Corinthians 3:17, ESV)

Now, I know many of you have been trying and trying for years, but you're just not sure if you're discerning correctly. I hope what you are about to read will cause you to stop beating yourself up and doubting and receive the freedom of the Spirit of the Lord.

Trial and Error.

"And they went through the region of Phrygia and Galatia, having been forbidden by the Holy Spirit to speak the word in Asia. And when they had come up to Mysia, they attempted to go into Bithynia, but the Spirit of Jesus did not allow them."

(Acts 16:6–7, ESV)

"Then they passed through Phrygia and the Galatian region, having been forbidden by the Holy Spirit to speak the Word in Asia. And having come down to the borders of Mysia, ***by a trial-and-error method*** *they kept on attempting to discover whether it was right to go to Bithynia. But the Spirit of Jesus did not permit them to do so.*

(Acts 16:6–7, WUESTNT)

Over the years, I have been asked who in the Word of God do I relate to the most. My answer is the apostle Paul. So you can imagine when I learned that the great apostle Paul had to learn spiritual discernment by exercising his senses through trial and error. I figured if that was Jesus' method for him, then it was good enough for me.

We all have heard the saying, practice makes perfect. You've just learned by the Word of God, that as you are faithful to live in communion, Holy Spirit will be faithful to make you proficient to discern the spiritual realms of good and evil.

After equipping thousands of business owners in over a hundred nations on how to live in communion with God Holy Spirit, I can tell you by experience, many of you are already discerning better than you know. So trust that it's Holy Spirit living in you, and it's no longer you who is living in that tent. (2 Corinthians 5:4)

Chapter 11

Endgame

"So we are convinced that every detail of our lives is continually woven together to fit into God's perfect plan of bringing good into our lives, for we are his lovers who have been called to fulfill his designed purpose."

(Romans 8:28, TPT)

As you've been reading this, you know I have made a big deal about life circumstances. They have been so key for me to understand the Word of God and my life with the abiding presence of Jesus Christ in communion with Holy Spirit.

So what I'm about to tell you may surprise you.

"It is never about the life circumstances!"

One afternoon when studying in communion with Holy Spirit, I was putting together teaching for a lesson I was going to teach. Out of nowhere Holy Spirit told me. "You need to know what the endgame is?"

In that moment, I couldn't imagine how this had anything to do with the subject I was going to teach. As I sat there trying to recall where I read about the endgame in the Bible, I came up with nothing. Then I asked the Lord, "What is the endgame?" He said, "I've already revealed it to you." As I sat there for a bit, pondering what in the world is the endgame, I still got nothing. Then Holy Spirit led me to John 17:20–23, an area of Scripture He knew I loved very much as I have highlighted and underlined them with four different colors.

"I do not pray for these alone, but also for those who will believe in Me through their word; that they all may be one, as You, Father, are in Me, and I in You; that they also may be one in Us, that the world may believe that You sent Me. And the glory which You gave Me I have given them, that they may be one just as We are one: I in them, and You in Me; that they may be made perfect in one, and that the world may know that You have sent Me, and have loved them as You have loved Me." (John 17:20–23, NKJV)

In the most challenging times, we all have prayed and renewed ourselves in Romans 8:28. In the thick of things, we have cried out, Lord, I love you, and I know all life circumstances work together for my good according to your purpose. Today I am sharing with you what that purpose is: It is the endgame.

The ENDGAME for Holy Spirit is for all believers and those who will be reconciled to God through Jesus Christ to become perfect and united in Christ, just as He and the Father are perfectly one. This way, the world will know that the Father has sent Jesus Christ and loves every individual just as He loves His Son.

Based on my personal experience, I understand that life can be both difficult and exhilarating. That's why I find The Passion Translation of Romans 8:28 to be particularly encouraging. It helps us recognize God's love in the midst of all life circumstances.

Now that you understand, God Holy Spirit directs every aspect of our lives, both as individuals and as a collective body, towards the ultimate goal of reaching perfection in Jesus Christ, just as He and the Father are perfectly one. As you move forward, I pray you approach all of life's situations with a heart filled with love for God, no matter the circumstances.

Chapter 12

Restoring Kingdom

As you know, I love my mornings with Holy Spirit. And in the early days, as He took me through the Word of God, there were subjects that intrigued me. One of those subjects was Kingdom. Jesus made statements such as: "What is the kingdom of God like?" " To what shall I liken the kingdom of God?" (Luke 13:18, 20) I did not understand these parables, they were confusing to the point of interesting, so interesting that I started seeking to know what they met.

Now let's fast forward 28 years to the present day. I have never stopped seeking to understand the wisdom of the Kingdom of God. And it was only six years ago, as I was preparing to teach on the subject in our Jesus Christ's CEOs Bible Institute, I came to one of my greatest revelations and understanding. Let me share a little bit of that with you.

"Your kingdom come. Your will be done
On earth as it is in heaven." (Matthew 6:10, NKJV)

We have all prayed this prayer a 1000 times. I want to bring your attention to this portion" "on earth as it is in heaven." As it is in heaven is the standard the Father wills on earth.

Saints, as you live in communion with God Holy Spirit, Jesus' standard in heaven is the standard He wills for everything that encompasses your life.

All authority in heaven has been given to Jesus, the kingdom of heaven is the kingdom of Christ. Jesus rules His domain and has dominion over all the citizens and their activities in the Kingdom of Heaven. Now, let me be bold and unapologetic, this is the standard Jesus wills on earth, and He especially expects it with those of us who already belong to His Kingdom, the body of Christ, His Church! (Colossians 1:15–18)

"To God our Savior, Who alone is wise, Be glory and majesty, Dominion and power, Both now and forever. Amen."
(Jude 25, NKJV)

If you were wondering if that is true, this verse in the letter of Jude clears that up.

The word "now" is defined as 'the present moment in time'. Now I know someone's asking themselves, Okay then, 'what is *Dominion*?' I'm glad you asked.

Dominion is Jesus Christ's manifest presence that directs and governs His entire domain. **Manifest** means to make clear to the eyes, mind, and senses.

Maybe you have witnessed what I have experienced. The Church, the body of Christ, often uses terms and phrases from the Bible as buzzwords and slogans without actually understanding their true significance. One such word is "Kingdom." Because those in the body of Christ do not fully comprehend what it means when they use it in various contexts. It is not backed up by the evident power from on high. Why? Because it does not meet Jesus' standard in heaven.

Restore: Bring back to an original condition or a place of departure.

We do not need to look any further than "dominion" to see why Holy Spirit does not manifest Jesus' authority and power in His Church. Christians today have not been crucified with Christ, they still live carnally unto themselves. They are not willing to forsake all to become authentic disciples of Jesus Christ. (Luke 14:25–33, Galatians 2:20)

"Living in Communion" with Holy Spirit is intended to bring about the restoration of Jesus' dominion, ruling and reigning His Church. It aims for Holy Spirit to manifest in the body of Christ, Jesus' authority and power as were evident in the Church's original design. (Luke 24:49, Acts 1:8)

Over the years, I have prayed with great faith, bold prayers, and big prayers. Six years ago, I started praying this prayer every day. For me, there has never been a bigger prayer and a more transforming prayer than this one. I pray it becomes your heart and daily prayer as it is for me.

Prayer

Lord, I know I don't fully know what I ask, but as a man after your own heart, I'm asking. (Mark 10:38–39)

Lord, I am asking for your dominion, manifest presence to direct and govern my entire body, heart, mind, soul, and spirit in Jesus' name Amen.

If you truly pray this prayer as a man or woman after Jesus' own heart, then watch out, your life will never be the same. I say this from experience. It will be exceedingly and abundantly so much better!

Chapter 13

Where is "communion of the Holy Spirit" in the Bible?

Where is *"communion of the Holy Spirit"* in the Bible? That was my very question to the Lord one morning when He was speaking to me through a vision.

Let me first give you the back story. The last six years of our business were very difficult as the Lord was teaching me and perfecting me as the new man. In year 18 of our business, my mom cried out to God, "Lord, I don't want the company anymore." Very quickly and in dramatic fashion, the Lord brought an end to the company my Mom dedicated to Him, and in turn, He gave to her.

Mom retired, and I was ready to launch a new company with Jesus. So as Mom did, I thought I better dedicate the company to Jesus before launching it. Then while still in my study and prayer closet, I thought, "Lord, I'm going to go a little further than that, and I am going to make a personal covenant with you."

"Lord, I have tasted the best this world has to offer and don't desire more of the same. Therefore, I make this covenant with you. 'Time is precious, the Lord's work is much, I will not spend my time doing any other business that is not the work of the Lord.'"

When making this covenant with Jesus, my heart was right, but I didn't fully understand what I was doing, nor did I know Jesus was going to take me up on it by changing the trajectory of my life. When I made my covenant, I thought I was dedicating myself and the new business to the Lord, but the Lord had different plans.

Now that I had made a covenant giving Jesus unconditional and unrestricted use of my life, He was now going to use me with thousands of Christian companies throughout the world instead of being the CEO of one company. It was while making this covenant in January 2001 that Holy Spirit said, "I want you to establish a Storehouse for Jesus, His companies, and His CEOs", and then gave me the name 'Windows of Heaven' Jesus' Storehouse. (Malachi 3:6–12)

"And it shall come to pass afterward That I will pour out My Spirit on all flesh; Your sons and your daughters shall prophesy, Your old men shall dream dreams, Your young men shall see visions."

(Joel 2:28, NKJV)

Over the next few months, Holy Spirit gave me visions regarding Jesus' Storehouse. Here is one of the first ones. This vision was related to taking me out of business and putting me into full-time ministry. The Lord was showing me well-known ministries, movements, revivals, and mega-churches. Then He showed me how you don't hear about them anymore. My interpretation in the moment was that the Lord was putting me into something that was going to fail before I ever even got started. I was angry and told the Lord, I don't want anything to do with ministry, I am going to stick with business. After a few minutes, I settle down and ask the Lord, why don't you hear about these ministries or movements anymore? His response was, **"Because none of them led My people into communion with the Holy Spirit."** I had gone through the Bible a few times and could not immediately recall this phrase. So, I said, "Okay, Lord, where is that in the Bible?"

I had the first edition of Logos Bible Software and opened up the search tool, searching through the New King James Version as that was the version I was reading in that season of my life. I discovered only one result in the whole entire Bible. It was the apostle Paul's closing prayer to the church in Corinth.

"The grace of the Lord Jesus Christ, and the love of God, and ***the communion of the Holy Spirit*** *be with you all. Amen."*

(2 Corinthians 13:14, NKJV)

As I mentioned earlier, Jesus was changing the trajectory of my life. He was putting me into full-time ministry, and with this vision, Holy Spirit made very clear that whatever the ministry was going to be, the activities we were going to do, every single one of them must be anchored in leading the Lord's people into communion with God Holy Spirit. This is one of those authoritative communications from God over the years where I have said,

"YES Sir!"

Other Bible translations use the word fellowship instead of communion. Holy Spirit knew I was reading from the NKJV and therefore used the word communion. Whatever translation you are using, they all define communion or fellowship as participation. Here is the sense of what communion means.

Communion

The act of joint participation in activities (the life of Christ) with Holy Spirit. (Galatians 2:20) An intimate fellowship (relationship) with Holy Spirit. (1 Corinthians 6:19)

In the next section, you're going to see that I didn't realize in this vision that this was the lifestyle Jesus Christ had already accomplished in my life. And what you have been reading here in "Living in Communion" is how Jesus had Holy Spirit do it with me.

" Then Peter opened his mouth and said: "In truth I perceive that ***God shows no partiality****. But in every nation whoever fears Him and works righteousness is accepted by Him."*
(Acts 10:34–35, NKJV)

I believe with great conviction that Jesus shows no partiality. That which He has done with me, He will do for anyone who turns to Him (as I have done) with all of their heart. "Living in Communion" with Holy Spirit is the biblical path on how to do that.

Saints, consider yourself led!

Authentic Disciples

Making You An Authentic Disciple

Chapter 14

Make Disciples

Holy Spirit continued to give me vision and direction for Windows of Heaven Jesus' Storehouse. One morning He said, “I want you to make disciples.” My response was, "Lord, I have not gone to school for that. I have not been trained on how to make disciples, I'm a businessman, how in the world do you do that?"

Holy Spirit responded, ***"How have I done it in your life?"***

Funny story but true, I said, "Lord, this would've been really good information to have six or seven years ago. If I knew you were going to have me make disciples, I would've kept better track of how you were doing things in my life so that I could teach others." His ways are not our ways, so true.

My Mom and I were in the gourmet beef jerky business. Our company was birthed from my Mom making beef jerky for my Dad. Back 40 years ago, Mom was the first person who launched preservative and nitrate-free beef jerky into the mainstream snack food industry! Today that is the standard for all products.

My point in telling you this is that Mom had a recipe, and when the product was produced in our factory by our 250 employees according to the recipe, the end result was amazing. We never could make enough product when the Lord's hand and favor was upon us. Imagine if we didn't give our factory team members a recipe! what do you think our customers would've gotten?

I think you get the point. And that's when the Holy Spirit said to me, "You need to define what a disciple of Jesus Christ is. If you can't define them, you can't make them. If you can't define them, my people don't know what I am making them into."

This sent me on a journey with Holy Spirit for almost one year.

I studied and then studied more. I wrote out a statement and refined it more times than I want to remember. And then Holy Spirit had me settle on this definition.

An authentic disciple is a person who habitually lives a self-sacrificial life abiding in the living person of Jesus Christ. Baptized with power, a disciple lives an experiential lifestyle in *communion with the Holy Spirit, manifesting mighty acts of love, faith, gifts, and signs, confirming their discipleship.

***Communion is a person's participation in the presence of the Holy Spirit as He manifests the Spirit of Jesus Christ in their mortal flesh.**

You may be asking yourself why do I use the word authentic? Here's why. I have discovered that the greatest hindrance in making disciples of the Lord's people is that the church-going Christian already believes they are a disciple. If this were genuine, then Holy Spirit wouldn't have to include two chapters ago, 'Restoring Jesus's kingdom, His dominion ruling His Church.'

Here's how I'm gonna wrap up this section of living in communion. I'm going to break down this authentic disciple description into five small individual lessons. I'm going to strengthen you in this description with God's Word. Then I am going to extend an invitation to you to make a written covenant with "Jesus" to habitually live as an authentic disciple through communion *(participation)* with God Holy Spirit.

'Living in Communion' Journal

As you already know, Holy Spirit is using my life and how He made me into an authentic disciple as a pattern for you. So from this point forward, I always want you to have a 'Living in Communion' journal. (Philippians 3:17)

As you go through these five brief lessons, go back and follow the pattern of reading, seeking, meditating, exercising, experiencing, and discerning Holy Spirit's revelation of the ENDGAME He desires to be made perfect in you.

If you're ready, grab a bible and your journal, and let's go.

Chapter 15

Study Guidelines

Before we get started with the first lesson of an authentic disciple, I want to give you a very simple study flow. Don't underestimate the simplicity, as you get started with this, the revelation will be more than you can handle. If that is not the case, pray John 14:26 as you open up the Word of God. As you master this flow and want to go exceedingly and abundantly farther in your Bible study than you can possibly imagine. *I encourage you to get yourself Logos Bible software.* https://www.logos.com/

I also am going to go easy on you and give you one week, seven days to study each subject. The impartation of revelation and your transformation is more important than the information.

Bible Reading

In each of these lessons, I will give you a few verses. This will be one translation, then I want you to read the same scriptures from two other translations, it doesn't matter what they are.

These verses will have bible cross references. I want you to look up and read every one of them in your favorite translation.

Anything and everything that stands out to you, I want you to put in your 'Living in Communion' journal. It won't be everything you read. Look for those Holy Spirit-revealed nuggets each day.

Keywords

I will give you a couple of keywords for each lesson. I want you to look up their definitions with a regular dictionary. Then I want you to write them in your 'Living in Communion' journal.

Meditation

Now that your 'Living in Communion' journal is full of information regarding the subject, I want you to meditate on what's in your journal.

The first distinction is your journal is not supposed to be filled with just information. More importantly, I want it filled with revelation that comes from your time of meditating in communion with God Holy Spirit.

This means that after you have spent your time meditating on a subject, I want you to journal what you saw, heard, and pondered in your time of meditating in communion with Holy Spirit. ***Your journal is a place for you to record what you believe God Holy Spirit is communicating to you.***

Another distinction, your journal is not a place to tell God what you know. He already knows, He gave it to you. (John 3:27) Your journal's a place for you to record by faith what you believe Holy Spirit has been talking to you about. Do you see the difference?

This would be a great time to go back and read again the chapter on meditation in communion with Holy Spirit.

Recapping the Flow

- Read the Bible
- Journal versus Holy Spirit highlighted for you
- Keyword look-up and record the definitions
- Meditate
- Record Holy Spirit's communications

From here, I will let you go back and review what takes place next. Here's a hint. Belief Exercise.

OK, it's time to jump into our first lesson.

STORE

Get your custom 'Living in Communion' journal at our jcceos.com STORE.

Chapter 16

Self-Sacrificial Life

Authentic Disciple Description

An authentic disciple is a person who *habitually lives a self-sacrificial life* abiding in the living person of Jesus Christ. Baptized with power, a disciple lives an experiential lifestyle in *communion with the Holy Spirit, manifesting mighty acts of love, faith, gifts, and signs, confirming their discipleship.

***Communion is a person's participation in the presence of the Holy Spirit as He manifests the Spirit of Jesus Christ in their mortal flesh.**

With this lesson, I am going to exhort you to habitually live a self-sacrificial life according to the Word of God.

Please read these verses and their cross-references and journal the few verses Holy Spirit highlights for you.

"And he who does not take his cross and follow after Me is not worthy of Me. He who finds his life will lose it, and he who loses his life for My sake will find it."

(Matthew 10:38–39, NKJV)

Forsake All

"Now great multitudes went with Him. And He turned and said to them, "If anyone comes to Me and does not hate his father and mother, wife and children, brothers and sisters, yes, and his own life also, he cannot be My disciple. And whoever does not bear his cross and come after Me cannot be My disciple. For which of you, intending to build a tower, does not sit down first and count the cost, whether he has enough to finish it—lest, after he has laid the foundation, and is not able to finish, all who see it begin to mock him, saying, 'This man began to build and was not able to finish Or what king, going to make war against another king, does not sit down first and consider whether he is able with ten thousand to meet him who comes against him with twenty thousand? Or else, while the other is still a great way off, he sends a delegation and asks conditions of peace. So likewise, whoever of you does not forsake all that he has cannot be My disciple."

(Luke 14:25–33, NKJV)

"Those who have ears to hear, let them hear!"

Living Sacrifice

"I APPEAL to you therefore, brethren, and beg of you in view of [all] the mercies of God, to make a decisive dedication of your bodies [presenting all your members and faculties] as a living sacrifice, holy (devoted, consecrated) and well pleasing to God,

which is your reasonable (rational, intelligent) service and spiritual worship."

(Romans 12:1, AMP)

Crucified

"I have been crucified with Christ; it is no longer I who live, but Christ lives in me; and the life which I now live in the flesh I live by faith in the Son of God, who loved me and gave Himself for me."

(Galatians 2:20, NKJV)

Define These Keywords

Forsake
All
Sacrifice
Crucified

Meditate

These verses not only communicate that you must offer yourself daily but, more importantly, that you should offer yourself once for all time unconditionally and permanently as an acceptable living sacrifice. Paul says it's reasonable for God to ask you to habitually live your life as a bondservant to Jesus Christ for His glory and unrestricted use.

Authentic discipleship has and always will cost an individual their life. I know 'self' (the control of one's life) is probably the hardest and most fearful thing to let go of. Meditate on living habitually as a living sacrifice, dead unto yourself, giving Jesus, from this day forward, unrestricted use of your life, regardless of the outcome.

Journal, what you saw, heard, and pondered in your time of meditating in communion with God Holy Spirit.

Chapter 17

Abiding In The Presence of Jesus

Authentic Disciple Description

An authentic disciple is a person who habitually lives a self-sacrificial life *abiding in the living person of Jesus Christ.* **Baptized with power, a disciple lives an experiential lifestyle in *communion with the Holy Spirit, manifesting mighty acts of love, faith, gifts, and signs, confirming their discipleship.**

***Communion is a person's participation in the presence of the Holy Spirit as He manifests the Spirit of Jesus Christ in their mortal flesh.**

With this lesson, I want to awaken you to the reality of the abiding living presence of Jesus Christ in you through communion with the Holy Spirit.

After the cross, resurrection, and sending of the Holy Spirit, a disciple's relationship transitions from being an external following to an internal abiding. Authentic disciples abide in the Spirit of the living God, a spiritual union of one: the Spirit of God in them and them in the Spirit of God. (John 4:23-24, 17:20–23) An authentic disciple's reality is no longer "What would Jesus do?" but rather "What is Jesus doing?" (John 5:19)

Please read these verses and their cross-references and journal the verses Holy Spirit highlights for you.

"At that day you will know that I am in My Father, and you in Me, and I in you."

(John 14:20, NKJV)

"But you are not in the flesh but in the Spirit, if indeed the Spirit of God dwells in you. Now if anyone does not have the Spirit of Christ, he is not His."

(Romans 8:9, NKJV)

"Do you not know that you are the temple of God and that the Spirit of God dwells in you?"

(1 Corinthians 3:16, NKJV)

"And what agreement has the temple of God with idols? For you are the temple of the living God.
As God has said: 'I will dwell in them And walk among them. I will be their God, And they shall be My people.'"

(2 Corinthians 6:16, NKJV)

"Therefore let that abide in you which you heard from the beginning. If what you heard from the beginning abides in you, you also will abide in the Son and in the Father."

(1 John 2:24, NKJV)

Define These Keywords
Abide
Presence
Temple
Dwell

Presence

Jesus promised never to leave you (John 14:16, 14:18)
Jesus dwells with you NOW! (John 14:17)
Jesus is in you NOW! (John 14:17)
Jesus is upon you NOW! (Act 1:8)
Jesus makes His home with you NOW! (John 14:23)

Meditate

Cultivating a consciousness of presence is something I spend a lot of time on in my own life. Living from a reality that Jesus Christ, the living God, is present at all times and in every circumstance is a game changer for the body of Christ to live as mighty disciples. Please, I cannot emphasize enough to get into the daily practice of cultivating a reality of knowing the presence of Jesus Christ in you. Living from a conscious reality of His presence will absolutely change everything in the Church as we know it today!

Journal, what you saw, heard, and pondered in your time of meditating in communion with God Holy Spirit.

Chapter 18

Communion of the Holy Spirit

Authentic Disciple Description

An authentic disciple is a person who habitually lives a self-sacrificial life abiding in the living person of Jesus Christ. Baptized with power, a disciple *lives an experiential lifestyle in *communion with the Holy Spirit,* **manifesting mighty acts of love, faith, gifts, and signs, confirming their discipleship.**

***Communion is a person's participation in the presence of the Holy Spirit as He manifests the Spirit of Jesus Christ in their mortal flesh.**

With this lesson, I want to share with you right from the Word of God how you practically maintain and participate in what pertains to Jesus Christ through communion with God Holy Spirit.

"The grace of the Lord Jesus Christ, and the love of God, and **the communion of the Holy Spirit** be with you all. Amen."
(2 Corinthians 13:14, NKJV)

Communion

The act of joint participation in activities (the life of Christ) with Holy Spirit. (Galatians 2:20) An intimate fellowship (relationship) with Holy Spirit. (1 Corinthians 6:19)

Please read these verses and their cross-references and journal what Holy Spirit highlights for you.

Pertains to Jesus

"I have yet many things to be saying to you, but you are not able to be bearing them now so far as your understanding and receiving of them is concerned. However, whenever that One comes, the Spirit of the truth, He will lead you into all the truth, for He will not speak from himself as a source, but as many things as He hears He will speak, and the things that are coming He will make known to you. That One shall glorify me, because He shall take out from that which ***pertains to me*** *and make it known to you. All things, as many as the Father has, are mine. On this account I said that He takes out from that which* ***pertains to me*** *and shall make it known to you."*

(John 16:12–15, WUESTNT)

"Jesus is the door, and communion with Holy Spirit is the key that opens it"

Maintain a Living Communion

"I, in contradistinction to anyone else, am the vine, the genuine vine, and my Father is the tiller of the soil. Every branch in me not bearing fruit He takes away. And every branch bearing fruit, He cleanses it in order that it may keep on bearing more fruit. As

for you, already you are cleansed ones because of the word which I have spoken to you. ***Maintain a living communion with me,*** *and I with you. Just as the branch is unable to be bearing fruit from itself as a source unless it remains in a living union with the vine, so neither you, u****nless you maintain a living communion with me.*** *As for myself, I am the vine. As for you, you are the branches. He who* ***maintains a living communion with me*** *and I with him, this one is bearing much fruit, because apart from me you are not able to be doing anything. If anyone is not* ***maintaining a living communion with me,*** *he was thrown outside as the branch is and was caused to wither. And they gather them and into the fire they throw them, and they are burned. If you* ***maintain a living communion with me*** *and my words are at home in you, I command you to ask, at once, something for yourself, whatever your heart desires, and it will become yours. In this my Father is glorified, namely, that you are bearing much fruit.*

So shall you become my disciples."

(John 15:1–8, WUESTNT)

Joint-Participation

"Faithful is God through whom you were divinely summoned into a ***joint-participation*** *with His Son, Jesus Christ our Lord."*

(1 Corinthians 1:9, WUESTNT)

Define These Keywords
Pertain
Maintain
Living
Summoned

Meditate

As we learned in the Abiding lesson, the disciple relationship transitions from being one in the flesh (follower) to being one in union with the Spirit of Jesus Christ. So it is natural to conclude that by joining these two lessons together, it is impossible to live as an authentic disciple of Jesus Christ apart from habitually living a lifestyle in communion with Holy Spirit.

Journal, what you saw, heard, and pondered in your time of meditating in communion with God Holy Spirit.

Chapter 19

Mighty Acts

Authentic Disciple Description

An authentic disciple is a person who habitually lives a self-sacrificial life abiding in the living person of Jesus Christ. Baptized with power, a disciple lives an experiential lifestyle in *communion with the Holy Spirit, *manifesting mighty acts of love, faith, gifts, and signs, confirming their discipleship.*

***Communion is a person's participation in the presence of the Holy Spirit as He manifests the Spirit of Jesus Christ in their mortal flesh.**

One of the names of Jesus is: "Mighty God." (Isaiah 9:6). When the Spirit of God dwells in a person as His temple, He does not void any of His authority or attributes as Mighty God. In fact, authentic disciples are also known as mighty disciples.

Please read these verses and their cross-references and journal what Holy Spirit highlights for you.

Mighty God

"In mighty signs and wonders, by the power of the Spirit of God, so that from Jerusalem and round about to Illyricum I have fully preached the gospel of Christ."

(Romans 15:19, NKJV)

"Truly the signs of an apostle were accomplished among you with all perseverance, in signs and wonders and mighty deeds."

(2 Corinthians 12:12, NKJV)

"Since you seek a proof of Christ speaking in me, who is not weak toward you, but mighty in you."

(2 Corinthians 13:3, NKJV)

"And what is the exceeding greatness of His power toward us who believe, according to the working of His mighty power"

(Ephesians 1:19, NKJV)

Mighty Acts

"Most assuredly, I say to you, he who believes in Me, the works that I do he will do also; and greater works than these he will do, because I go to My Father."

(John 14:12, NKJV)

"But you shall receive power (ability, efficiency, and might) when the Holy Spirit has come upon you, and you shall be My witnesses in Jerusalem and all Judea and Samaria and to the ends (the very bounds) of the earth."

(Acts 1:8, AMP)

Confirming An Authentic Disciple

"And these signs will accompany those who believe: in my name they will cast out demons; they will speak in new tongues; they will pick up serpents with their hands; and if they drink any deadly poison, it will not hurt them; they will lay their hands on the sick, and they will recover."

(Mark 16:17–18, ESV)

"So then the Lord Jesus, after he had spoken to them, was taken up into heaven and sat down at the right hand of God. And they went out and preached everywhere, while the Lord worked with them and confirmed the message by accompanying signs."

(Mark 16:19–20, ESV)

Define These Keywords

Mighty
Signs
Confirm
Accompany

Beyond Imagination

"Now to Him who is able to do exceedingly abundantly above all that we ask or think, according to the power that works ***in us.****"*

(Ephesians 3:20, NKJV)

Did you catch that? You have an opportunity by the power that works "in you" to participate in supernatural acts that are so far beyond anything you can imagine, ask or think!

Mediate

We all need a greater reality of the infinite power of Jesus Christ that abides in us. In your time of meditation, let the Holy Spirit reveal and purge areas of unbelief. Then start exercising bold acts of faith, believing the Lord to confirm them with accompanying signs.

Journal, what you saw, heard, and pondered in your time of meditating in communion with God Holy Spirit.

Chapter 20

Jesus Christ Manifested

Authentic Disciple Description

An authentic disciple is a person who habitually lives a self-sacrificial life abiding in the living person of Jesus Christ. Baptized with power, a disciple lives an experiential lifestyle in *communion with the Holy Spirit, manifesting mighty acts of love, faith, gifts, and signs, confirming their discipleship.

***Communion is a person's participation in the presence of the Holy Spirit as** *He manifests the Spirit of Jesus Christ in their mortal flesh.*

We have reached the last lesson for our authentic disciple description. In this lesson, I want to share with you how authentic disciples participate with God Holy Spirit as He manifests Christ in their mortal flesh/body.

Please read these verses and their cross references and journal what Holy Spirit highlights for you.

Manifest

*"I have been crucified with Christ; it is no longer I who live, **but Christ lives in** me; and the life which I now live in the flesh I live by faith in the Son of God, who loved me and gave Himself for me."*

(Galatians 2:20, NKJV)

*"For I know that this will turn out for my deliverance through your prayer and the supply of the Spirit of Jesus Christ, according to my earnest expectation and hope that in nothing I shall be ashamed, but with all boldness, as always, so now also **Christ will be magnified in my body**, whether by life or by death."*

(Philippians 1:19–20, NKJV)

*"But we have this treasure in earthen vessels, that the excellence of the power may be of God and not of us. We are hard-pressed on every side, yet not crushed; we are perplexed, but not in despair; persecuted, but not forsaken; struck down, but not destroyed—always carrying about in the body the dying of the Lord Jesus, **that the life of Jesus also may be manifested in our body.** For we who live are always delivered to death for Jesus' sake, that **the life of Jesus also may be manifested in our mortal flesh**."*

(2 Corinthians 4:7–11, NKJV)

Define These Keywords

Vessels

Life

Magnified

As we learned from these scriptures, one of the functions of Holy Spirit is to reveal Jesus Christ to the world. (John 15:26, 16:14,

Acts 1:8) As temples of the Holy Spirit, authentic disciples receive authority to participate with the Holy Spirit as He manifests the Spirit of Jesus Christ in their mortal bodies. (1 Corinthians 6:19-20)

Manifest is defined as: "to make clear or obvious to the eyes, mind, and senses."

How?

Authentic disciples live self-sacrificial lives dead unto themselves, so it is no longer they who live but Christ living in them. In this manner, Jesus becomes preeminent (the first), and the authentic disciple is simply a joint participant as Holy Spirit manifests the life of Christ in their mortal flesh.

It's in this manner that authentic disciples make clear and obvious to the world that it's no longer they who live, but it's Christ living in them.

Meditate

"He must increase, but I must decrease."

(John 3:30, NKJV)

As you meditate on these Scriptures, think about what it will take for more of the fullness of Jesus Christ to tangibly manifest in your mortal body. Less of you and more of Him.

Journal, what you saw, heard, and pondered in your time of meditating in communion with God Holy Spirit.

Chapter 21

Enlist My People

By now, you have learned that Holy Spirit has asked me to do many things that I have no prior knowledge or experience in. Shortly after making authentic disciples in communion with Him, He did it again. In one of my quiet times with the Lord, He said, *"I want you to build Me an army."* And as you know by now, I responded "Lord, I have never been in the military, I know nothing about it. How do you build an army?" As I sat there waiting for His response, *He said, "the first thing you need to do is to enlist My people."* Again I said, "OK, where is that in the Bible?"

"And the things that you have heard from me among many witnesses, commit these to faithful men who will be able to teach others also. You therefore must endure hardship as ***a good soldier of Jesus Christ****. No one engaged in warfare entangles himself with the affairs of this life, that he may* ***please him who enlisted him as a soldier.****"*

(2 Timothy 2:2–4, NKJV)

Today it is estimated that there are approximately 2.6 billion Christians in the worldwide population of about 8 billion people. These are people who confess Jesus Christ as their Lord and Savior. But did not necessarily agree to their enlistment (summons) to jointly participate with Him as a good soldier of Jesus Christ, also known as authentic disciples.

With Holy Spirit's command to build Him an army, He was telling me "I want you to build me an army of authentic disciples who will live in agreement with My enlistment." Like the apostle Paul, through trial and error, I discerned that the Lord wanted me to enlist His people to live in covenant with Him as authentic disciples.

*"Now **it is in my heart to make a covenant with the Lord God** of Israel, that His fierce wrath may turn away from us."*

(2 Chronicles 29:10, NKJV)

***"Then they entered into a covenant to seek the Lord God** of their fathers with all their heart and with all their soul;"*

(2 Chronicles 15:12, NKJV)

*"Then Jehoiada **made a covenant** between himself, the people, and the king, **that they should be the Lord's people**."*

(2 Chronicles 23:16, NKJV)

*"Then the king stood by a pillar and **made a covenant before the Lord**, to follow the Lord and to keep His commandments and His testimonies and His statutes, with all his heart and all his soul, to perform the words of this covenant that were written in this book. And **all the people took a stand for the covenant**."*

(2 Kings 23:3, NKJV)

Covenant: a contractual agreement between God and a person. *(for an expanded word study see Strong, G1242)*

"For this is My blood of the new covenant, which is shed for many for the remission of sins."

(Matthew 26:28, NKJV)

In business, we have a term known as bait and switch. It's a broad term, so let me use it in this way. For example, I put out a job advertisement making a job opportunity look so sweet that the candidate accepts the position. But when they start working, they learn there were a lot of things they weren't told about the job before accepting it.

When Holy Spirit gave me an understanding of what an authentic disciple is, I realized that many of our altar calls are a form of bait and switch. We have told people the beautiful truth of the love of Christ to receive eternal life but neglected to tell them all they were agreeing to as enlisted soldiers of Jesus Christ.

Many people like to treat the cause of an illness rather than the actual illness. I am not one of those people. As I mentioned before, It's estimated that there are 2.6 billion Christians in the world today, but nobody would ever agree that even 80% of them are living as authentic disciples, as I have defined here in Living in Communion. This is why the Lord said, you need to first enlist My people.

What I love about the Lord's command to build Him an army is that in His mercy and compassion, He already calls the 2.6 billion

His people. So please join me in enlisting His people to habitually live as authentic disciples through communion *(participation)* with God Holy Spirit.

As I mentioned before, I am going to extend an invitation to you to make a written covenant with Jesus Christ to habitually live from this day forward as an authentic disciple. But to stay true to who I am, I am begging you to first count the cost.

Let me recap what I want you to consider before making a covenant with Jesus Christ. I have defined for you an authentic disciple. I have equipped you on how you must live as an authentic disciple. Now the time has come for you to thoroughly count the cost and forsake all to habitually live in covenant as an authentic disciple of Jesus Christ through communion with God Holy Spirit. (Luke 14:25–33), (Galatians 2:20)

So here's what I want you to do. I want you to get your 'Living In Communion' journal ready, and I want you to write out a personal covenant, a love letter to Jesus Christ. But before, as you know, I have been enlisting the Lord's people for quite some time, so let me give you a few examples (for your understanding) of the covenants that have been made by other authentic disciples in our Jesus Christ's CEOs Bible Institute.

Actual Covenants with minor edits to honor confidentiality

I enter into this covenant with Jesus Christ. To enlist in His army, to live as an authentic disciple. To be an obedient and loyal soldier in whatever it is the Lord asked me to do. To live, according to the Word of God, by the power of the Holy Spirit. To sacrifice my life and my will for His purpose and plans in all matters. To glorify

Him and serve Him with all that I have and all that I am. So help me, God.

Today I commit my life to live as an authentic disciple who habitually lives a self-sacrificial life abiding in the living person of Jesus. I commit to living a life in communion with the Holy Spirit, manifesting mighty acts of love, faith, gifts, and signs confirming my discipleship. Holy Spirit, help me live in communion with you daily, listening and obeying your commands to what you will ask me to do. Help me to intentionally spend time with you, and may my communion with you overflow to my sphere of influence for the advancement of your kingdom on earth. Amen

Today I voluntarily make a covenant with My Lord Jesus Christ to live as an Authentic Disciple, to effectively change my status from being of this world to being a citizen of the kingdom of God to live a self-sacrificial life abiding in the living person of Jesus Christ. To serve and to be fruitful by teaching others. To be an example to others and to fully commit myself and all which the Lord provides for my course to His Kingship. As I commit myself may the Lord be my guide and strength in this new journey in which I have willingly placed myself as a partner with the Lord and learn from those who first entered into this journey before me.

I voluntarily commit to being Your authentic disciple and walking boldly in communion with the Holy Spirit for the rest of my life. I will seek You first in all things and obey Your instruction. I will go where You send me, with strength and courage, to reclaim territory in Your name, knowing that You are leading the way. Through communion with the Holy Spirit, I will participate in mighty acts to display Your love on this earth. I declare that I am second, and

You are first. I commit to glorify You, disciple others, and build Your Kingdom on earth. My life is not my own, and I submit to Your perfect will. If I live, I live to the Lord, if I die, I die to the Lord. Whether I live or die, I am the Lord's.

I commit to living my life as an authentic disciple of Jesus Christ. Let this document serve as a line drawn in the sand today that, from now on, I vow to live a life of joyful surrender to the King of Kings. I will continue to listen to the leading of the Holy Spirit for my life, family, and business. I willingly release the reins of my life to the One who knows far better than I do. I acknowledge that I will speak what He speaks, go where He goes, and do what He does. Let anyone to reads this understand and fully support my devotion to fulfilling this commitment.

I solemnly and irrevocably, with boundless joy and celebration, make this covenant with Jesus Christ the Most High God, who lives in me and I in Him. On this day, I give up my life to enter into new life as a citizen and soldier of God's Kingdom—one of Christ Jesus' holy people. My new life's purpose is to do the will of God, directed by His Holy Spirit, without delay or disagreement, in all things. I fearlessly declare that I am sanctified—set apart from the world, unto God—from this day until I leave the world to join My King in heaven.

I understand that many laws, regulations, and Kingdom customs will govern my conduct and require me to do things under this agreement that a person of this world does not have to do. My enlistment is more than an agreement, it's a lifestyle that will transform every aspect of my life. It affects a change in status from a person of this world to a Citizen of the Kingdom of God. Once executed, the authority of Jesus Christ and the power of the Holy Spirit will be bestowed unto me by the Father, and I will be accountable for every word and deed. I may, without my consent, be ordered to give up everything I want and have to follow HIM and HIS WAYS. I do hereby acknowledge to have voluntarily enlisted. I certify that I have carefully read this document. I do solemnly swear (or affirm) that I will support and defend the Word of God and His AGENDA for the earth against all enemies, foreign and domestic; that I will bear true faith and allegiance to the same; and I will obey the orders of the Father, the Holy Spirit, and Jesus Christ, and the orders of those He appoints to shepherd me on the earth, according to regulations and the code of Righteousness, Justice, Truth, Hope, and Love. So help me, God.

Heavenly Father, with bowed knees and reverent heart, I pledge to restore the preeminence of Jesus Christ in MY life and hereby write this covenant to live my life as an authentic disciple. (Colossians 1:18) I dedicate my entire life to you. I will live a self-sacrificial life centered on the living person of Jesus Christ. I have been baptized with your power, and I am choosing to live an experiential lifestyle in communion with my gift, the Holy Spirit, so that the Spirit of Jesus Christ can be made manifest in my mortal flesh. I will demonstrate my discipleship via powerful acts of love, faith, gifts, and signs. I commit to not only living as a disciple but also raising up other disciples in accordance with your great commission. I accept my inheritance as your child and hereby commit to playing my part as your ambassador, creating authentic communities, occupying the given territory, and ultimately revealing the fullness of your Kingdom.

My Enlisting Covenant. I completely and fully surrender my life, now and into eternity, to the total Lordship of Jesus Christ, not merely as His servant, but as a co-laborer to prepare and release the kingdom of heaven on earth. I, therefore, surrender all my past and current earthly desires to my Supreme Commander, Jesus Christ, so He can refill me with His desires and destiny for me, which He designed before time began. I furthermore pledge my absolute loyalty only to His kingship for the family, business, ministry, and spheres of influence He has given to me, only doing what I see Him doing before and through me, enthusiastically engaging in His desired path for my life, and proclaiming to all the glory He deserves for what He wills to accomplish through me. In covenant of His blood running through my veins unto His glory forever,

I'm mindful Lord Jesus of Your Love and Grace. I'm undeserving but truly blessed. God the Father loved His children so much that He sent You to His earth. You, born of the Virgin Mary, sinless, grew as a baby, toddler, infant, adolescent, pre-teen, teen, and young man into a man. You experienced all things human. Good, bad, hurt, pain, joy, temptation, and humiliation. More importantly, not excluding torment, anguish, and feeling you have been forsaken by God the Father. But You knew the price had to be paid to save God the Father's Children and me. My cost to be Your Authentic Disciple will never amount or come to the cost You paid for my soul. You willingly and lovingly paid the price to save my soul. You are my Savior!

So I enter this covenant. Lord, I am Yours. You paid the price for me. I owe You everything. I declare, "all is yours." You, Lord, are in control. I am to be about Your work. Your Great Commission sends me so Your Holy Spirit may work through me and draw others to You. May I fulfill, with the help of Your Holy Spirit, the way and life of an "Authentic Disciple." I enlist today, this very moment.

I desire to be an Authentic disciple for You. May Your Holy Spirit guide and direct my path. In faith, I believe You will make all things prosper in Your Will. May the message, "It's not about me," be clear. May Your Holy Spirit's work through me shine bright and grow Your Church and Kingdom. May I joyfully look toward the day where Your Kingdom reaches the point where it is time for You, My Lord, to return and call me home. Bless my walk as I work for You. Amen!

Invitation

Well, I could do this all day as our Jesus Christ's CEOs Bible Institute to date has enrolled business owners from 105 nations and have received covenants like these from over 50 nations. I love reading these love letters to Jesus. Why do I call them that? Because Jesus said, there is no greater love than one who lays down their life for another. (Mark 12:31) These saints have laid down their lives, demonstrating their love for another, Jesus Christ!

Now it's your turn if you are so willing. So again, I urge you to first count the cost. By voluntarily making a covenant, you are making an irrevocable agreement with Jesus Christ to live as an authentic disciple, and as such, you are effectively changing your status from a person of this world to a citizen of the kingdom of God.

'Living in Communion' has served to inform those who would enlist in Jesus's army.

Call to Action

Saints, I invite you to voluntarily make your personal written covenant with Jesus Christ today.

Love Letters

If you went ahead and made your written covenant with Jesus Christ, would you please share your love letter with our ministry team? They love to be encouraged as they work faithfully and tirelessly in fulfilling the great commission. (Matthew 28:18–20)

You can share your covenant with our team at jcceos.com or livingincommunion.org

Thank you so very much!

Chapter 22

'Living *in* Communion' Fellowships

Windows of Heaven Jesus' Storehouse is a shepherding ministry for Christian business owners, their company's teams, and spouses. Our Jesus Christ's CEOs Bible Institute is the equipping arm of Jesus' Storehouse. Our JC CEOs Bible Institute's method of making authentic disciples of Jesus Christ is to lead the Lord's people into *living in communion* with God Holy Spirit. (Ephesians 4:11–13) JC CEOs**MEDIA** ministry's mission is to tell the world what Jesus is doing in business.

Local Communities

"The grace (favor and spiritual blessing) of the Lord Jesus Christ and the love of God and the presence and fellowship (the communion and sharing together, and participation) in the Holy Spirit be with you all. Amen (so be it)."

(2 Corinthians 13:14, AMP)

Jesus demonstrated through His first 12 disciples that being an authentic disciple of Christ is a continuous process that involves being part of a local community of believers. At Windows of Heaven, we call ours 'Living in Communion' fellowships.

"And they continued steadfastly in the apostles' doctrine and fellowship, in the breaking of bread, and in prayers. Then fear came upon every soul, and many wonders and signs were done through the apostles. Now all who believed were together, and had all things in common, and sold their possessions and goods, and divided them among all, as anyone had need. So continuing daily with one accord in the temple, and breaking bread from house to house, they ate their food with gladness and simplicity of heart, praising God and having favor with all the people. And the Lord added to the church daily those who were being saved."
(Acts 2:42–47, NKJV)

'Living *in* Communion' Fellowships

1. 'Living *in* Communion' Institute Fellowships

These ongoing weekly Institute fellowships equip "Business Owners" on how to participate with Holy Spirit intentionally in the comprehensive Business as ONE in Christ's Blueprint. Our blended learning of the Word of God and the experiences of one another doing business as authentic disciples in communion with Holy Spirit is what makes our Institute fellowships so appealing to CEOs.

2. 'Living *in* Communion' Company Fellowships

These weekly "company" fellowships (church/ekklesia) equip team members and the company's spheres of influence to habitually live and do business *(their trade)* in participation with God Holy Spirit as authentic disciples of Jesus Christ. Owners, your teams are not being equipped in this manner. So if you/we don't do it together, no one else will. *"And the things that you have heard from me among many witnesses, commit these to faithful men who will be able to teach others also."* (2 Timothy 2:2, NKJV)

3. 'Living *in* Communion' Spouse Fellowships

These weekly Spouse fellowships make authentic disciples who participate as a family with God Holy Spirit, creating a culture of the kingdom of Christ at home and in their neighborhoods. Since God Himself made spouses *(men and women)* one flesh, we believe He wants them included. Genesis 2:24

ENDGAME (John 17:20–23)

As you have learned, there is a fullness of Christ that JC CEOs, their teams, and spouses will never attain to this side of the new heaven and earth. Until the restoration of all things, there is always a greater fullness, individually and as one Body, that must be pursued in being made perfect in Christ, as He and the Father are perfectly one. Owners, will you and your company join us in this pursuit of Jesus' ENDGAME?

'Living in Communion' App

As of this writing, Windows of Heaven is just starting to build our independent and fully branded private community app. The app is intended to bring our various global 'Living in Communion' Fellowships together as ONE body of authentic disciples of Jesus Christ.

Your Call to Action

Dear Business Owners/CEOs and Spouses,

Have you ever experienced the fellowship of 'Living *in* Communion' with other covenant partners of Christ? It is unlike anything you have ever experienced before. The commitment to Jesus and to one another is incomparable to anything you have ever experienced with other communities.

Owners,

If the idea of 'Living in Communion' fellowships appeals to you, we invite you to take the first step and enroll in our Jesus Christ's CEOs Bible Institute. Our equipping will give you the tools to operate a company consecrated to Jesus and deepen your relationship with Him. Plus, it's completely FREE! Visit jcceos.com to learn more and join us soon.

Blessings,

The JC CEOs Bible Institute Team

JESUS CHRIST'S CEOs®

BIBLE INSTITUTE

Dear Christian Entrepreneurs and CEOs,

If you are seeking to be set apart as a distinct difference, as described in (Galatians 2:20), we invite you to enroll for FREE in the JC CEOs Bible Institute.

As a participant, you will receive an impartation from the Holy Spirit, gaining a greater revelation of Jesus Christ and your holy calling to oversee a for-profit business belonging to the kingdom of Christ on earth. (Matthew 6:10).

We look forward to helping you on your journey as a faithful and successful Christian business owner. (Acts 8:30–31)

Blessings,

The JC CEOs Bible Institute team

JC CEOs MEDIA

JC CEOs Media's mission is to proclaim to all the world the name and power of Jesus and all that He *(Jesus)* is doing in business. (Romans 9:17)

JCCEOS.TV

tv JC CEOs

JC CEOs Podcast

STORE at jcceos.com

Our personalized products are a great way to promote unity within Team Jesus. We take pride in providing high-quality swag items that devoted Saints are excited to wear or display on their desk.

Living *in* Communion

Authentic Disciples

From Self-Centered to Communion to Worldwide Ministry

As a former Business Owner, the Lord blessed Leray in business, he was honored twice as an elite CEO/entrepreneur by Inc. magazine, Merrill Lynch, and Ernst & Young. Not living for Christ at the time, Leray was living his dream and building a kingdom unto himself. But as you can read in 'Living in Communion', Mom and Dad, Leray's business partners, prayed this simple but powerful prayer.

"Lord, do whatever it takes to bring Leray into a personal relationship with you."

In 'Living in Communion,' you will learn how Jesus answered Mom and Dad's prayers. Leray takes you on his gut-wrenching journey from not living for Christ, nor reading the Bible, or even knowing that there was a Holy Spirit and shows you how the Holy Spirit led him into a revelatory and intimate relationship with Jesus Christ through communion (participation) with God Holy Spirit.

Leray Heyne's journey from living and conducting business from a self-centered carnal perspective to being launched by Holy Spirit into the worldwide ministry of Jesus Christ's CEOs is a biblical path for leading the universal Church into Communion with God Holy Spirit. 2 Corinthians 13:14

Leray Heyne is the Founder of Windows of Heaven Jesus' Storehouse, Jesus Christ's CEOs Bible Institute, and JC CEOSMEDIA- a worldwide ministry for Christian CEOs and Entrepreneurs at jcceos.com. As former CEO, Leray was honored twice as an elite CEO/Entrepreneur by Ernst Young, Inc. Magazine, and Merrill Lynch. Leray and his wife, Teresa, of 42 years, live in Orange County, CA.

$12.95
ISBN 978-1-7322947-1-4
51295>
9 781732 294714